Digger's Busy Day

Written by Amelia Marshall

Illustrated by Dan Bramall

W

FRANKLIN WATTS
LONDON•SYDNEY

It's busy at the building site
as the sun starts to rise.
Digger **CLUNKS** and **CLICKS**
as it stretches to the skies.

BRRR

Now there's lots of noise.
Digger's friends are all awake.
Trucks and tippers all start up,
rattle, **RATTLE**, shake!

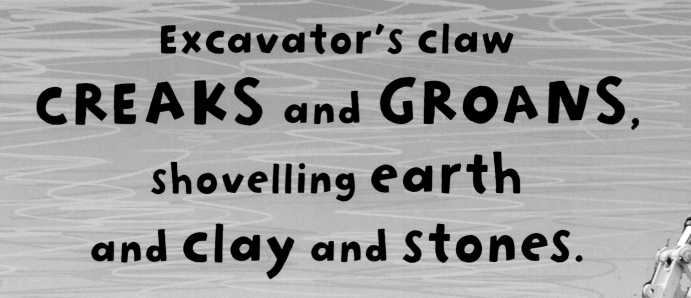

Excavator's claw
CREAKS and **GROANS**,
shovelling **earth**
and **clay** and **stones**.

Dump truck **HEAVES** the waste away, carrying **Sand**, **Concrete** and **Clay**.

Busy little bulldozer,
SQUASHES all the mud.
Its caterpillar tracks go
THUD! THUD! THUD!

Big yellow digger
swoops UP and DOWN!
Whoosh
shoots the mud,
all dusty and brown.

13

Front loader scoops up
the gravel in its teeth,
thick black tyres
CRUNCHING
underneath.

CRINKLE

Cement mixer churns,
imagine the **SOUND**
as it spins the **cement**
round and **round** and **round**.

Big long crane truck,
heavy hook **SWINGING**,
stretchy and strong,
metal chiming
and **RINGING!**

SWISH

19

Digger lifts its bucket,
tipping and tumbling,
earth and mud spilling,
piles of dirt rumbling!

21

Mighty tip-up truck
flings out its load,
thundering and **dumping**
by the muddy road.

Log truck stretches
its big metal claw,
gripping tree trunks
with a mighty
ROAR!

24

Steam roller **flattens** the road to shiny black, **pounding** the ground with **sticky** tarmac.

At the end of the day,
as the sun starts to set,
Digger is still **CHUGGING**,
the work's not over yet!

ZZzzz

Digger's friends slowly stop,
whirring softly one by one.
"Sshhh" go their engines
beneath the setting sun.

Truck terms

Bucket – allows the digger to scoop up and carry loads.

Teeth – part of the bucket, these cut into the ground.

Crawler tracks – spread weight so the digger doesn't sink in the mud.

Lugs – bumps in the tyres which help to grip.

Cab – where the driver of the truck or digger sits.

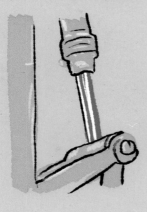

Pump – this helps the parts of the digger or truck move about.

Blade – bulldozers have a blade at the front to gather and push soil along.

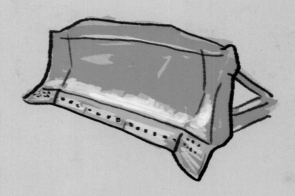

Grab – log trucks use this for lifting up logs.